ROQUE

DALTON

POEMS

translation:
Richard Schaaf

CURBSTONE PRESS

The poems in this collection are selected from the following books:

  La Ventana en el Rostro (Mexico, 1961)
  El Turno del Ofendido (Havana, 1963)
  Taberna y Otros Lugares (Havana, 1969)
  Las Historias Prohibidas del Pulgarcito (Mexico, 1974)
  Poemas Clandestinos (EDUCA, Costa Rica, 1976)

"Quito, February 1976: I Light the Fire and Beckon It"
by Eduardo Galeano
copyright © 1983 by Monthly Review Press
Reprinted by permission of Monthly Review Press.

          "Letter to Nazim Hikmet" first appeared in
                    THE MINNESOTA REVIEW.

Published with the support of the Connecticut Commission on the Arts, a State agency whose funds are recommended by the Governor and appropriated by the State Legislature.

I wish to thank Pamela Korsmeyer and James Scully who helped make this book possible: "Muchas gracias."

cover photo: kurt records

ISBN   0-915306-45-X   (cloth)
ISBN   0-915306-43-3   (paper)

06725

Curbstone Press
321 Jackson Street
Willimantic, CT.
06226
USA

POEMS

from **THE BANNED HISTORIES OF TOM THUMB (1974)**

from **CLANDESTINE POEMS (1975)**

Dear Jorge:

I came to the revolution by way
of poetry.
You can come (if you so desire,
if you feel you must) to poetry
by way of revolution. Therefore
you have an advantage. But
remember, if there was ever a
special reason why my company
in the struggle made you happy,
then in some small way you should
be grateful to poetry as well.

LETTER TO NAZIM HIKMET

1

Comrade Nazim:

this morning I recall your house in Peredelkino
resembling the heart of the forest, among gigantic pines,
I remember the ample fraternity of your antarctic eyes,
your crystalline poetry.

I take care of your gifts: the colorful
wooden spoon and the picture of Lenin
and I hope the awesome clay head from Izalco
that I left in your hands
speaks to you often about my poor country
and its bitter bread.

Comrade Nazim: I write this
from the neighborhood of sudden dread
from the Fifth Cell Block in the Central Penitentiary
of El Salvador.

I couldn't do this before when I was free
because feeling playful and bubbly at liberty one cannot
raise words to the high occasion of prisoners,
the old prisoners who, like you, showed the way
to see prison as one more tiny step of stone
on the road to winning a little of the future freedom for everyone.

2

They've held me prisoner, comrade, for nineteen days now.
The same ones who brand the dark rose, heart of our country,
with red-hot irons and acids,

who stole my freedom as though it were simply an object
and surrounded me with hatred, guards and walls
and took from me the currents of the wind,
the stars, the streets, the eyes of girls,
the downpours of these latitudes
that look for the fire in our flesh.

And here I am, with the poor murderer in spite of himself,
with the thief, the rapist, and the ignorant one,
sharing our daily mire and insults,
mingling our breathing with the usual outcries from behind
bars,
watching the days pass like exhausted swallows, pathetic
wings,
accused of anything for having loved hope and defended life
and having begun to be a man once and for all
going all out
barely pausing to examine
my apparent conceit, as it turned out.

When do I get out of here? It doesn't matter.
What does is that in spite of the hatred, the pain,
the uncertainty,
we must follow with firmness in the footsteps of the heart,
always joined in the struggle, facing hope,
and happy, very happy, very happy . . .

Pardon my confused expression and ideas:
there's a touch of fever and anxiety
between my crazed hands and brain;
what's more, according to the news
other comrades have been arrested . . .
I enclose some poems from these last days,
where friends speak from their cells,
only some of them, there are three hundred and twenty of us.
Will you give my regards to Memet? And you
take good care of your heart.

Especially today when America
has many doorways for you and your poetry.

I won't take up any more of your precious time
—has the snow melted yet in Moscow?—
and I close these lines with an embrace.

So long. May we keep on
hauling up the morning.

January, 1960

SOLIDARITY

You can't get out of your cell.
The bars
are dark, heavy.

But don't give up, no.
You can't get out
but between those cold iron bars
all the love in the world comes through . . .

YOU'VE BEATEN ME

You've beaten me badly
your brutal fist in my face
(naked and chaste
as a flower where spring
dawns)

You've locked me up even more
with your furious eyes
my heart dying of cold
under the avalanche of hate

You've scorned my love
laughing at its small, bashful gift
not wanting to understand the labyrinths
of my tenderness

Now it's my turn
turn of the offended after years of silence
in spite of the screams

Be quiet
be quiet

Listen

GEOGRAPHER

History is a pit
inhabited by pale looking guys
who drove themselves as though they were earthquakes

by orangutans in full-dress uniform
who had their portraits done alongside great, blue lakes

by the sick to their stomachs
who blotted out the formation of estuaries
and residual mountains

by savvy seductive little whores
who make you forget the splitting apart of plateaus
the death of solemn forests

by the dusty, sullen peoples
whose uproar drowns out
the presence of the sea

MEXICO

In the name of crushed bone
bits of lime mixed with dust
in the name of the blind who resist
the sun from down in their pit
In the name of the angel of crisis
of whoever despairs behind bars
in the name of the hungry oppressed
those who lost track of their steps

In the name of the dog that died
up against your cold, bitter thirst
in the name of the fire on which your
deeply wounded snowdome rests

In the name of the bone-dry tree
remembering its hanged bodies
in the name of the worm-eaten scream

In the name of the abysmal man
who, from his torn flesh, multiplies and swarms over you

MY NEIGHBOR

He has a rather plain wife.

He has two boys who drive him out of his mind
who these days chase the cats all over the neighborhood.

He works, reads a lot, he sings in the mornings,
and he asks after the ladies;
he likes bread *and* the baker,
he usually drinks
beer at noon;
he knows his soccer, he loves the sea,
he'd like to have his own car,
he goes to concerts, he has a small dog,
he has lived in Paris, and he's written a book—I believe
it was poetry—
he relaxes by watching the birds,
he pays his bills at the end of the month,
he helped repair the belfry . . .

Now he's in prison:
he's also a communist, so they say . . .

TWO GREEK GUERRILLAS:
AN OLD MAN AND A TRAITOR

(to the memory of Nikos Kazantzakis)

Panayotaros never put roses in his gun.

He refused to bury his first ambush victims
as was the custom:
he left them forever orphans of the cross
while the cruel sun laughed sharpening its claws.

Back then there was plenty of raw wine and hard cheese
and at night Demetrios, the baker,
would play his little guitar
at wild dances.

Panayotaros left us when the famine hit
and even the snakes began dying at our feet.
Now he's probably a minister or some such thing
judging by the respect with which all the doctors
pronounce his name in this horrible
hospital of outcasts.

THE GUILTY ONES

If you, dear School Presidents,
Faculty Doctors,
noble Magistrates, Ministers,
papa and mama,
Lieutenant-Colonels
had joined in your time
the Communist Party
(and stayed in)
I'd still be in something
such as the Christian Democratic Party.

But now I have no choice.
And I don't deny that this tremendous responsibility
occasionally makes me nervous!

When I met you, you were so punctilious, solemn . . .

REVOLUTION

"If they want my blood, I give them my blood . . ."
—Popular song

Blood and more blood raised from dust
its old cry its tumultuous cry
raised the sweaty banner under the sun
burned its bare foot its sandal
its skin stinking of salt
a furious gunbelt defended
dragged its horse its guitar
its taciturn sweetheart
its fresh memories
and its rage of a strong proud man
along the old ingratitude of the earth.

Now it is sleeping
an old man drunk on *pulque*
its shotgun getting rusty
in a corner, nosed about by pigs.

GENERAL MARTÍNEZ

They say he was a good President
because he allotted cheap housing
to the Salvadorans who were left . . .

60% OF EL SALVADOR

For $140,000
you can scratch your back
with Brancusi's *Bird in Space.*

Just $17
and you'll receive *Fortune* magazine
for twelve months.

Poor peon
who barely makes $55 a year:
the worth of modern sculpture
is an unresolved matter,
and *Fortune*
comes out only in English,
so why kid yourself?

May eternal spring be with you, compatriot
of our Central American soccer (junior division) champions!

ARS POETICA
to Raúl Castellanos

Anguish exists.

Man uses his old disasters as a mirror.

Barely an hour after dark
that man picks up the bitter scraps of his day
painfully places them next to his heart
and sweating like a consumptive who still hasn't given up
sinks into his deep, lonely room.
Here, such a man chainsmokes
he concocts disastrous cobwebs on the ceiling
he loathes fresh flowers
his own asphixiating skin exiles him
he stares at his cold feet
he believes his bed is his daily grave
his pockets are empty
he's hungry
he sobs.

But those men, those other men,
gladly bare their chests to the sun
or to murderers on the prowl
they lift the face of bread out of ovens
like a benevolent flag against hunger
they laugh so hard with the children even the air hurts
they fill with tiny footsteps the bellies of blessed women
they split rocks like stubborn fruit in their solemnity
naked they sing into the refreshing glass of water
they joke around with the sea playfully taking it by the horns
they build melodious houses of light in windswept wildernesses
like God they get drunk everywhere
they settle with their fists against despair

their avenging fires against crime
their love of unending roots
against the atrocious scythe of hatred.

Anguish exists, yes.

As does despair
crime
or hatred.

For whom shall the voice of the poet speak?

TERRIBLE THING

My tears, even my tears
have grown hard.

I who believed in everything.
In everyone.

I who only wanted a little tenderness,
which costs no one nothing
but heart.

Now it's too late.

Now tenderness isn't enough.

I've had a taste of gunpowder.

LATIN AMERICA

The poet face to face with the moon
inhales his thrilling little daisy
takes his dose of foreign words
soars off on misty brushstrokes
scratches his little violin
    like a pederast.

Until he smashes his face
against the harsh wall of a barracks.

BAD NEWS ON A SCRAP OF NEWSPAPER

Today when my friends die
only their names die.

How can one aspire, from this violent pit,
to take in more than newsprint,
the splendor of delicate blacks,
arrows into our deepest memories?

Only those living outside of prison
can honor the dead, wash away
the pain of their deaths with embraces,
scratch gravestones with fingernails and tears.

Not prisoners: we just whistle
hoping the echo drowns out the news.

LOOKING FOR TROUBLE

The night of my first cell meeting it was pouring rain
Four or five characters out of the world of Goya
were very impressed with the way I dripped
Everyone there seemed somewhat bored
perhaps from the persecution and the daily nightmares
    of torture.

These somewhat hoarse-sounding organizers of labor unions
and strikes told me I'd have to
find a pseudonym
that I was going to have to pay five pesos a month
that we had to agree to do this every Wednesday
and how were my studies going
and for today we were going to read a pamphlet by Lenin
and that it wasn't necessary to say 'comrade' every minute.

When we broke up the rain had stopped
Mother scolded me for coming home late.

SOLDIER'S REST

The dead grow more intractable every day.

Once they were obedient:
we gave them a stiff collar a flower
we eulogized their names on an Honor Roll:
in the National Cemetery
among distinguished shades
on hideous marble.

The corpse signed up pursuing glory
once more joined the ranks
marched to the beat of our old drum.

Wait a minute!
Since then
they have changed.

These days they grow ironic,
ask questions.

It seems to me they realize that more and more
they are the majority!

The President of my country
is called for the moment Colonel Fidel Sánchez
    Hernández.
But General Somoza, President of Nicaragua,
also is President of my country.
And General Stroessner, President of Paraguay,
is also a little the President of my country, though
    less
than the President of Honduras, namely
General López Arellano, and more than the President
    of Haiti,
Monsieur Duvalier.
And the President of the United States is more
    President of my country
than the President of my country,
that one who, as I said, is for the moment
called Colonel Fidel Sánchez Hernández.

REVISIONISM

Never.

Because,
for example,
in Macao
the opiate of the people
is opium.

HEADACHES

It is beautiful being communist,
though it brings on many headaches.

And the communist headache
is supposed to be historical, meaning
it will not give way to aspirin
but only to the realization of Paradise on earth.
That's how it is.

Under capitalism our head throbs
and they decapitate us.
In the struggle for the revolution
the head is a time-bomb.

In building socialism
we plan the headache
which doesn't make it go away, on the contrary.

Communism will be, among other things,
as aspirin big as the sun.

AN OTTO RÉNE CASTILLO OF THE LAST CENTURY

Mateo Antonio Marure, precocious Guatemalan student,
received his B.A. in Philosophy when he was eleven
    being fully competent
in Theology when he was 14
took his Masters in Philosophy at 16
and at 22 (in 1810) his Doctorate in Philosophy
    and Law

Young leader of the independence movement
he went to San Salvador to raise those spirits
    left crushed
by the defeat of 1811
inciting the residents of Mejicanos to insurrection

At the time of his arrest for agitating in Guatemala
Captain-General José Bustamente testified against him:

that he was one of the most restless, seditious spirits
    in all the Province
obsessed with subversive ideas, never ceasing
    for an instant
even in prison where he is now

that he was one of the advisers of conspiracy
sworn into the Convent of Bethlemites
who relied on him to carry out their
    infamous plots
using his widespread reputation for being proud
    and fearless

that the insults and excesses he had committed
    on the most solemn occasions
and the insolence of his writing and papers
demonstrated his incorrigibility and lunatic
    imagination
that, therefore, his stay in any part
    of the realm
where it was impossible to confine him without
    risking his escape to troubled countries
or his agitating others who were enjoying
    tranquillity
was now intolerable

Otto René I mean Mateo Antonio Marure
was deported to Spain when he was 29
leaving his wife and son behind

But on reaching Spanish Havana
he was sent into the Morro stronghold
and stricken by an endemic disease
he died in a Charity Hospital

If Colonel Carlos Arana Osorio
had been Captain-General by then
he wouldn't have allowed Otto I mean Marure
    to leave for Havana
but would have murdered him right there
in the anti-guerrilla headquarters in Zacapa
or in the 1st Corps Police Academy
or in one of the many secret apartments
the CIA keeps in Guatemala City for murdering
these shining lights of San Carlos University

MORAZÁN AND THE YOUTH

Given that he was the true father of our country
by shooting him they murdered also
our love for Central America.

In his last testament he said the youth are
the lifeblood of this country
(not the little old men of the Unionist Party
not ODECA
not don Napoleón Viera Altamirano
or General Idigoras Fuentes or Somoza
and neither SIECA nor AID).

Because, he added,
only the youth
would be able to follow his example of dying unshaken
before leaving Central America abandoned
to the disgraceful disorder in which it finds itself.

Referring to himself
he figured he would die poor and in debt
and his execution by firing squad would be murder.

The Salvadoran oligarchy minted its vengeance
stamping his beautiful, exalted profile
on every coin.

Thus
the youth would think the Morazánian voice
depended on fluctuations of the dollar
and is a means of exchange and trade
having more to do with the manipulations
of the Central American Common Market

than with battlefields
and naked machete charges
against the conservatives
and imperialists of all times.

SOVEREIGNTY

The Nicaraguan guerrilla
Augusto César Sandino
told the yankee officers
who had invaded Nicaragua:
"The sovereignty of a people is not negotiable;
it is defended with guns in hand."

At the time of the 1932 worker-peasant insurrection
    in El Salvador
the yankees and the English proposed
to General Maximiliano Hernández Martínez
the landing of troops in the port at La Libertad
to help him put down the rebellion.

General Martínez replied that that would jeopardize
    the national sovereignty
and he sent the admirals a telegram
which he, in turn, had received from General
    José Tomás Calderón,
better known as 'Turncoat,'
Chief of Operations of the Punitive Forces of the
    Salvadoran Government
in charge of Pacification of the Western Zone of the
    Republic.

The telegram went like this:

GREETING HONORABLE COMMANDERS WE DECLARE
SITUATION ABSOLUTELY UNDER CONTROL BY
GOVERNMENT FORCES OF EL SALVADOR. LIVES
PROPERTY SAFE. CITIZENS FOREIGNERS OFF STREETS
AND RESPECTING LAWS OF THE REPUBLIC. PEACE IS
ESTABLISHED IN EL SALVADOR. COMMUNIST OFFENSIVE

CRUSHED ITS FORMIDABLE CENTERS DISPERSED. AS OF
TODAY FOURTH DAY OF OPERATIONS FORTY-EIGHT
HUNDRED COMMUNISTS LIQUIDATED.

Martínez spent thirteen years defending the national
    sovereignty in this way.

In the last 40 years
12 new governments have passed from hand to hand
that tremendous responsibility.

ALL

We were all born half-dead in 1932
we survived but half-alive
each of us with an account of thirty thousand massacred
(yielding high interests
fat profits)
and that today manages to smear death on those who go on
    being born
half-dead
half-alive

We were all born half-dead in 1932

To be Salvadoran is to be half-dead
what is stirring there
is the half of life they left us

And as all of us are half-dead
the murderers regard themselves as not only totally
    alive
but also immortal

But they are also half-dead
living only by halves

Let's unite the half-dead who are the fatherland
that *we may call ourselves your children*
in the name of the murdered
united against the murderers of all
against the murderers of the dead and the half-dead

All of us together
have more death than they

but all of us together
have more life than they

The all-powerful union of our half-lives
of the half-lives of all those born half-
    dead
in 1932

THE CONSOLATIONS OF
SOUL SAVING

(1932)

Agustín Farabundo Martí,
letting it pass when the priest
with whom he had refused to confess
embraced him,
walked on to the execution wall.

Suddenly he turned
and called to Chinto Castellanos,
the Presidential Secretary, who had stayed up with him
    through the night
chatting and smoking cigars
in the room where the dead lie in state.

—Embrace me—he whispered in his ear—
it irritates me that the last embrace I take away
from life should be with such a scheming priest.
—And why me?—asked Chinto.
—Ah—replied Farabundo—because you are going to be
    one of us,
in time you'll see.

And he faced the firing squad.

II

(1944)

To execute Víctor Manuel Marín
they had to prop him up by his armpits
on wooden sawhorses
(those they put the ironing board on).

During the torture they broke his arms
and legs and a few ribs,
plus they tore out one eyeball
and crushed his testicles.

The same priest who couldn't get Farabundo to confess
went up to Víctor Manuel, and said:
'My son, I come to console your spirit.'

And that one replied between his busted teeth
and swollen lips:
'It's my body that weakens, not my spirit.'

Then they shot him.

III

(1973)

Every time I read in the society pages
of *Diario de Hoy* or *Prensa Gráfica*
those pompous obituaries
costing two hundred *colones* or more
informing us a bourgeois died
consoled with the last rites
of our Catholic religion,
I think of all those two deaths mean to us:
that they refused the consolations of those soul-savers.

REFLECTION

There are no 'mysteries' in History.
Only suppressions,
the lies of those who write History.

The History of the so-called 'soccer-war'
was written by the CIA and the Pentagon,
by the Intelligence Agencies of the Governments
of El Salvador and Honduras,
by penpushers for the oligarchies of both countries,
by ad agents for the manufacturers of Economic Integration,
by PR and Marketing experts on Central America,
by spineless and usually anonymous editorialists,
chroniclers and reporters
for the Great Isthmian Press (Radio & TV included)
by the Departments of Information & Psychological Warfare
of the High Commands united under CONDECA, etc. etc.

The falsification of the history of that war
is its continuation by other means
the continuation of the real war that develops
under the appearance of a war between El Salvador and
     Honduras:
the imperialist-oligarchical-bourgeois-governmental war
against the peoples of Honduras and El Salvador.

LOVE POEM

Those who widened the Panama Canal
(and were on the 'silver roll' not the 'gold roll')
those who repaired the Pacific fleet
in California bases,
those who rotted in prisons in Guatemala,
Mexico, Honduras, Nicaragua
for stealing, smuggling, swindling,
for starving,
those always suspected of everything
("Allow me to place him in your custody
for suspicious loitering
aggravated by the fact of being Salvadoran")
those who pack the bars and whorehouses
in every port and capital
('The Blue Grotto,' 'The G-String,' 'Happyland')
the sowers of corn deep in foreign forests,
the crime barons of the scandal sheets,
those who nobody ever knows where they're from,
the best artisans in the world,
those who were riddled with bullets crossing the border,
those who died from malaria
or scorpion bites or swarming bees
in the hell of banana plantations,
those who got drunk and wept for the national anthem
under a Pacific cyclone or up north in the snow,
the spongers, beggers, pot-heads,
the stupid sons of whores,
those who were barely able to get back,
those who had a little more luck,
the forever undocumented,
those who do anything, sell anything, eat anything,
the first ones to pull a knife,
the wretched the most wretched of the earth,
my compatriots,
my brothers.

POETICUS EFICACCIAE

You can judge
the moral bearing of a political system,
a political institution
a political man
by the degree of danger they attach
to the fact of being observed
through the eyes of a satiric poet.

ON SURPLUS-VALUE, OR
FROM EACH WORKER THE BOSS
ROBS TWO

Housework by the woman
creates time for the man
to do socially necessary work
for which he isn't fully paid
(the greater part of its value
the capitalist robs)
but only enough
so he can live and go on
working,
pay with which
the man returns to the house
and says to the woman
          ay, see what you can do
to stretch it out
enough to cover all the expenses
of the housework.

STATISTICS ON FREEDOM

Freedom of the Press for the Salvadoran people
costs 20 cents a day per head
counting only those who know how to read
and have more than twenty cents extra
after having managed to eat a little something.

Freedom of the Press for the big
retailers industrialists and ad agencies
is calculated at 1000-plus pesos a page in black & white
and I don't know how much per square inch
of text or illustration.

Freedom of the Press
for Don Napoleón Viera Altamirano
and the Dutrizes and the Pintos and the owners of *The World*
is worth several million dollars:
what the buildings are worth
built according to military specifications
what the presses and paper and ink are worth
their firm's financial investments
what they receive every day from the big
retailers industrialists and ad agencies
and from the government and the U.S. Embassy and
from other embassies
what they extract from the exploitation of their workers
what they get from blackmail ("For not publishing
the accusation against the very distinguished gentleman
or for publishing in the most timely manner the secret
which will sink the smallest fish to the sandy bottom")
what they earn from payment of rights on
"exclusives," for example
Love Towels are . . . Love Statues are . . .
what they take in daily
from each Salvadoran (and Guatemalan)
who has 20 cents extra.

According to capitalist logic
Freedom of the Press is just another commodity
and from its total value
each gets a share according to his (or her) ability to pay:
for the people twenty cents a day per head's worth
of Freedom of the Press
for Viera Altamirano Dutriz Pinto etc. etc.
millions of dollars a day per head's worth
of Freedom of the Press.

FOR A BETTER LOVE

"Sex is a political category."
—Kate Millett

Everyone agrees that sex
is a category in the world of lovers:
hence tenderness and its wild branches.

Everyone agrees that sex
is a category within the family:
hence children,
nights together
and days apart
(he, looking for bread in the street,
in offices or factories;
she, in the rearguard of household work,
in the strategy and tactics of the kitchen
allowing them to survive in the common battle
at least until the end of the month).

Everyone agrees that sex
is an economic category:
it's enough to mention prostitution,
fashion,
sections of the newspaper for her only
or only for him.

Where the trouble begins
is the moment a woman says
sex is a political category.

Because when a woman says
sex is a political category
she can cease being woman in itself

and begin being woman for herself,
constituting the woman in woman
starting from her humanity
and not from her sex,
conscious that magical lemon-scented deodorant
and soap that voluptuously caresses her skin
are made by the same corporation that makes napalm
conscious that the tasks belonging to the home
are tasks belonging to the social class to which that home
                                                    belongs,
that the difference between the sexes
shines much brighter in the deep loving night
when all those secrets that kept us
masked and strangers, become known.

THE POLICE
AND THE NATIONAL GUARD

Always they saw the people
as a heap of backs running away,
like a field to be beaten flat under clubs of hate.

Always they saw the people with the eye of a marksman
and between the people and the eye
was the sight of the pistol or the rifle.

(Once they too were people
but with hunger and unemployment as an excuse
they accepted a gun
a club and a monthly wage
to defend those who make hunger and unemployment.)

Always they saw the people enduring
sweating
shouting
holding up placards
raising fists
and, at most, telling them:
"Dirty bastards, your day will come."
(And with each passing day
they believed they'd made a good deal
betraying the people from whom they came:
"The people are a bunch of simple-minded wimps—
                                    they thought—
we did well by going over to the quick and strong.")

And then they had only to pull the trigger
and bullets rang out from the ranks of the police and the
                                                        Guard

against the ranks of the people
they always went that way
from there to here
and the people fell bleeding
week after week year after year
bones shattered
weeping through the eyes of its women and children
fleeing in panic
and ceased being the people having become a mob
every man for himself disappearing into the safety of his
own home
and then nothing
only the firemen hosing the blood from the streets.

(The colonels added their crowning touch:
"That's it boys—they told them—
beat those civilians over the head
fire on the rabble
you too are uniformed pillars of the Nation
first-rate priests
in the worship of the flag the national seal the anthem
the founding fathers
representative democracy the official party and the free
world
whose sacrifice won't be forgotten by the decent folk
of this country
though right now we can't give you a raise
as is, of course, our desire.")

Always they saw the people
convulsed in the torture chamber
hanged
beaten
broken
swollen
smothered
raped

eyes and ears pierced with needles
twitching from electric shocks
drowned in urine and shit
spat on
dragged
their last remains giving off spitting fumes
in the hell of quicklime.

(When the tenth National Guardsman was killed . . .Killed
                                                    by the people
and the fifth flunkey had his hair ruffled by the urban
                                                    guerrilla
the National Guard and their flunkeys started to wonder
mostly because the colonels had already changed their tune
and today they blame every defeat
on "subversive elements among our troops.")

Fact is the police and the Guard
always saw the people from there to here
and the bullets only went from there to here.
They had better think hard
they had better decide for themselves if it's too late
to search out the ranks of the people
and shoot from here
side by side with us.

They had better think hard
but meanwhile
they better not look surprised
much less be offended
if now a few bullets
start reaching them from this side
where the same people has always been
only this time we're coming head-on
and bringing more and more guns.

REMEMBRANCE AND QUESTIONS

Here in the University
while I listen to a speech by the President
(in each doorway there are state police
making their contribution to culture)
pale with disgust, I recall
the sad peace of my native poverty,
the gentle slowness of death in my village.

My father is waiting back there.
I came to study
the architecture of justice,
the anatomy of reason,
to look for answers
to the terrible abandonment, the thirst.

Oh night of false lights,
tinsel made out of darkness:
where should I flee
if not into my own soul,
soul that wanted to be a flag returning home
and that now they want to turn into a filthy rag
in this temple of thieves?

ARS POETICA 1974

Poetry
pardon me for having helped you to understand
that you are not made of words alone.

LIKE YOU

I, like you,
love love, life, the sweet delight
of things, the blue
landscape of January days.

Also my blood bubbles over
laughing through my eyes
which have known the rush of tears.

I believe the world is beautiful,
that poetry is, like bread, for everyone.

And that my veins don't end in me
but in the unanimous blood
of those who struggle for life,
love,
things,
countryside and bread,
poetry for everyone.

THE BIBLE BUSINESS

The Bible says
Christ multiplied loaves and fishes
for the people.

If he did that, he did good,
and that makes him greater than a great general
who won a thousand battles where millions of poor folks
died.

But at present the North Americans—
to keep the loaves and fishes from multiplying,
and so that everyone is resigned to putting up with
the widespread hunger which makes for big business—
these North Americans multiply the production of Bibles
in every language we poor folk speak
and ship them to us in the hands of fair-haired boys
who have been thoroughly trained by their Generals.

VARIATIONS ON A PHRASE BY CHRIST

"Render unto God the things that are God's
and unto Caesar the things that are Caesar's."

1

Render unto God the things that are God's
and unto the fascist government of President Molina
what belongs to the fascist government of Pres. Molina.

I don't pretend to know, from my limited perspective,
all that belongs to God

but, yes, I'm sure about what we ought to give
the fascist government of Molina.

2

Render unto God the things that are God's
and to the government of the rich
what belongs to the government of the rich.
But,
what more are we going to give the government of the rich
if, with the help of their government, the rich have already
stripped us of everything?

TWO RELIGIONS

When revolution appears on the horizon
the old cauldron of religion erupts.

In ordinary times
religion was going to mass,
paying tithes to the house of God,
baptizing children
and confessing sins to settle accounts with oneself.

When revolution appears on the horizon
the churches remember the masses,
descending on them from clouds and mysteries
and feudal tranquillity.

Fat-assed pastors talk about the end of the world
when what approaches is the end of exploitation;
hysterical prophets talk about choosing between Good and Evil
when the people need to take a stand
against oppression and hunger.

When social revolution begins unfurling its flags
the heirs of those who crucified Christ
tell us Christ is our only hope
precisely because he waits for us
up there in His Kingdom, which is not of this world.

This is the religion Marx called
"the opiate of the people"
because in that form it's just one drug more to stuff men's
heads with
keeping them from finding the way to social struggle.

But Camilo Torres, among others,
left us saying there's also a positive religion
that springs forth from the soul of revolution
like poems and hymns
and that it risks its life in *this* world
not after death.
In this religion serve men who are
(like true communists)
the salt of the earth.

WAYS OF DYING

Commander Ernesto Ché Guevara
called by pacifists
"the great adventurer of armed struggle"
went and applied his revolutionary concepts
in Bolivia. Testing those concepts out
he and a handful of heroes lost their lives.

The great pacifists of the prudent way
also tested their own concepts in Chile:
now more than 30 thousand are dead.

Imagine what the dead would say
on behalf of each of those concepts
if they could relate to us their experience.

OLD COMMUNISTS
AND GUERRILLAS

There have been good people in this country
ready to die for the revolution.

But the revolution everywhere needs people
who are ready not only to die
but also to kill for it.

About those good people Ché said:
"They are capable of dying in torture chambers
without letting out a single word,
but they are incapable of taking out
a machine-gun nest."

And the class enemy as is well known
uses not only torture chambers
to defend exploitation
but also machine-gun nests
and all sorts of such things.

In short:
only those who are ready to die and kill
will end up being people who are good
for the revolution.

Because it's through *them* the revolution will be made.

Though the revolution ends up being for
all good people.

ADVICE WHICH IS NOW NOT NECESSARY ANYWHERE IN THE WORLD EXCEPT EL SALVADOR

Don't ever forget
that the least fascist
among the fascists
are also
fascists.

CROCK LOGIC

"Criticism of the Soviet Union
can only be made by one who is anti-Soviet.

Criticism of China
can only be made by one who is anti-China.

Criticism of the Salvadoran Communist Party
can only be made by an agent of the CIA.

Self-criticism is equivalent to suicide."

PARABLE BASED ON REVISIONIST STUDY OF VOLCANOES

The Izalco volcano
as a volcano
was ultra-leftist.
It hurled lava and rocks from its mouth
and rumbled and made tremors,
breaking out against peace and tranquillity.
Today it is a good civilized volcano
which will coexist peacefully
with the *Hotel de Montaña del Cerro Verde*,
and we'll be able to put fireworks
in its big mouth like those our popular
representatives spew out.
Volcano for executives
and even for revolutionaries and trade unionists
who know how to stay put and who aren't hotheaded,
it will no longer be the symbol of nutty thundering guerrillas
who are the only ones who miss its geological outbursts.
Respectable and gentle proletarians of the world:
the Central Committee invites you
to learn the lesson of the Izalco volcano:
fire has gone out of fashion,
why then should we carry it
within our hearts?

ONLY THE BEGINNING

A friend, a poet of sorts,
defined the lament of
middle-class intellectuals this way:

"I am a prisoner of the bourgeoisie:
I can't help being what I am."
And maestro Bertolt Brecht,
communist, German playwright and poet
(in that order) wrote:
"What is robbing a bank
compared with the crime
of founding a bank?"

What I conclude from this
is: if, to transcend himself
a middle-class intellectual
robs a bank,
up to then he'll have done nothing
but get himself a hundred years of pardon.

HITLER MAZZINI:
COMPARISON BETWEEN CHILE
IN 1974 AND EL SALVADOR IN 1932

It doesn't surprise me that they slander
the honorable Military Junta of Chile.

Communists are like that:

They say the military has killed
in some four months
more than eighty thousand Chileans.

That's an exaggeration
since concrete evidence shows
no more than some
forty thousand were killed.

It was the same with El Salvador in 1932.
The communists say General Martínez
killed in less than a month
more than thirty thousand peasants.
That, too, is an exaggeration:
no more than twenty thousand were verified dead.

The rest
were considered disappeared.

YOU AND GOLD
AND WHAT'S IN STORE

Under capitalism one lies in saying:
"Take care of yourself, you're worth your weight in gold."
Because under capitalism the only ones
worth gold are the owners of gold.

In building socialism
one no longer lies, and it is said:
"You're worth more than gold, but
it's necessary to take care of
the gold all of society owns,
holdings are important."

Only under communism will it be said:
"You are worth what you are worth.
Gold has nothing to do with what you're worth.

Under communism gold's only value
is the use-value each worker and citizen gives it
for example, in dental work
in decorations
or in necklaces or earrings
for girls."

FOR THE RECORD

On behalf of those who wash others' clothes
(and wash from the whiteness others' filth)

On behalf of those who look after others' kids
(and sell their labor power
in the form of maternal love and humiliation)

On behalf of those who live in others' homes
(no longer a caring womb but a tomb or prison)

On behalf of those who eat another's crumbs
(and even as they eat feel like thieves)

On behalf of those who live in a foreign country
(the houses the factories the shops
the streets the cities the towns
the rivers the lakes the volcanoes the mountains
always belong to others
which is why there are police and watchmen
guarding them against us)

On behalf of those who have only
hunger exploitation sickness
thirst for justice and for water
persecutions prison terms
loneliness neglect oppression death

I charge private property
with depriving us of everything.

COULD BE

For the bourgeoisie
the fatherland laws honor and God
have no meaning without
private property and 'free enterprise.'

For proletarians
the death of private property
and 'free enterprise'
would give meaning to the fatherland laws honor
and, perhaps, even to God.

THE PETTY BOURGEOISIE

(one of its manifestations)

Those who
in most cases
want to make revolution
for History for logic
for science and nature
for next year's books or the future
to win arguments and even
to appear finally in the newspapers
and not simply
to put an end to the hunger
of those who are hungry
and the exploitation
of those who are exploited.

It is natural, then,
that in revolutionary practice
they only concede before the judgment of History
morality humanism logic science
books and newspapers
and refuse to concede the last word
to the hungry the exploited
who have their own history of horror
their own implacable logic
and who will have their own books
their own science
nature
and future

THE BIG BOURGEOISIE

Those who make rum
and then say it's not possible to raise the wages
of the peasants
because they'll go spend it all on rum.

Those who, within their own families,
speak English exclusively
among paintings by Dubuffet and Bohemian crystal
and life-size photographs of mares
brought from Kentucky and Vienna
and make us pay daily in sweat and blood
for their misery in having to wake up every day
in this country of filthy Indians
so far from New York and Paris.

Those who have understood that Christ
if you see things right
was really the Anti-Christ
(because of all that about loving one another
without distinction between the dregs and decent folk
and the bit about the early Christians conspiring
in the complicity of the catacombs
and the agitation against the Roman Empire
and the fish so similar to the hammer and sickle)
and that the true Christ was born in this century
and was called Adolph Hitler.

Those who vote in El Salvador
for the President-Elect of the United States.

Those who create a favorable atmosphere for
misery and malnutrition

which produces consumptives and the blind
and then build
sanitariums and rehabilitation centers for the blind
so as to exploit them
in spite of tuberculosis and blindness.

Those who have neither homeland nor nation here
but only property
bordering on Guatemala to the Northeast
Honduras to the North
The Gulf of Fonseca and Nicaragua to the Southeast
and the Pacific Ocean to the South
and on said property Americans have come
to set up some factories
where slowly but surely cities towns villages and cantons
have been springing up
full of brutes who work
and brutes armed to the teeth who don't work
but keep the brutes who work
in their place.

Those who tell the doctors the lawyers the architects
and agronomists and economists and engineers
know which side your bread is buttered on
and that each year it's necessary to make tougher Penal Codes
and hotels and casinos equal to those in Miami
and fifteen-year plans equal to those in Puerto Rico
and civilizing operations
consisting of removing blue blemishes from the asses
of distinguished ladies and gentlemen
and irrigation carrying everyone's few drops of water
exclusively to land where grows that good wood that gives such
good shade
above all to those who aren't professionally disposed
to carry a candle to the burials of so many foul-smelling
barefoot people.

Those who, to have Freedom of the Press
and constitutional rights,
bought newspapers, radio and TV stations
the whole works including journalists reporters and cameramen
and bought the political constitution and with it the
Legislative Assembly and Supreme Court.
Those who, to sleep safe and sound,
don't pay the block or neighborhood night watchman
but go directly to the Joint Chiefs of Staff
of the Armed Forces.
Those who
sure enough
have everything to lose.

HISTORY OF A POETIC

for E.S.

Well you see once there was this poet
from here, this country
who was no beauty he wasn't real bad either
like Satan (who he dreamt he was)
just sort of ugly and chicken-chested and a real nice guy
who had it rough finding time to write
between studying Bookkeeping
and working in the Courts.

Well, this national poet loved justice and women
(maybe he loved women a bit more than justice)
(but that's not so bad you should see
the shape justice is in around here)
and every other Saturday he wrote
sonnets to the people
to The Future That Shall Be
and to liberty for Tyrians and Trojans
all with a burning look in his eye
after having called corn, bread
and rum, wine.
So that was his life and work
which were talked about in the salons
of "La Masacuata"
and which even managed to get a
kind review from Roberto Armijo.

One day it happened that the price of paper
went through the roof:
and in the Courts as well as in the University
with no let-up they rationed sheets of paper to the poet
so he wouldn't waste them on anything that wasn't
his drab judicial job and his accounting apprenticeship.

Then one weekday quite a ways from Saturday
the poet started to see the light—
that behind the whole thing was a plot against poetry
that simply couldn't be put up with
for all the government would talk about was oil going up.

That was when he began writing on the walls
in his own handwriting
on fences and buildings
and on the giant billboards.
The change was no small thing
quite the contrary
in the beginning
he fell into a deep creative slump.

It's just that sonnets don't look good on walls
and phrases he was mad about before, like
"oh abysmal sandalwood, honey of moss"
looked like a big joke on peeling walls.

Furthermore, the night watchmen and informers
and the National Guard and their flunkeys
were going to come down on him anyway
(if they hadn't fingered him right off)
even if what he wrote on the walls were verses like
"glow, pale lamp, your face in my arms"
or
"I sipped the light of your cheek"
or
"there is no God nor Son of God without development."

So that's why the poet took the bull by the horns
and went into urban guerrilla warfare
ERP: Propaganda and Agitation Section
of the National Committee
for whom he now writes on walls:

"viva guerrilla warfare"
"armed struggle today—Socialism tomorrow"
"ERP"

And if anybody says this story is
schematic and sectarian
and that this poem is
a whole lot of drivel and that it fails
"precisely in that it exalts its own motives"
he can go fuck himself
because the story and the poem
are nothing less than the plain truth.

ROQUE DALTON

Roque Dalton was born in San Salvador, El Salvador in 1935. He studied law and social science at universities in San Salvador, in Chile and in Mexico.

In 1955, the same year he shared the Central American Poetry Prize with Otto René Castillo, Dalton joined the Communist Party.

He was imprisoned and forced into exile several times. Once, in 1960, he was arrested by the Lemus government and sentenced to be shot. But the government fell only four days before his scheduled execution. And again, while he was under sentence of death, an earthquake split the walls of his cell and Dalton escaped. For the next thirteen years he lived in exile: in Guatemala, Mexico, Czechoslovakia and Cuba. He also lived for a short time in North Vietnam.

In 1961 his first book of poetry, *La Ventana en el Rostro*, was published in Mexico, and he won the International Literature Prize awarded by the International Union of Students (UIE). In 1969, he won the *Casa de las Américas* Prize in Cuba for his book, *Taberna y Otros Lugares*.

In 1973, living in Cuba, Dalton decided to return to his own country and join the People's Revolutionary Army (ERP). Living underground as a guerrilla, he continued to write poetry and popular history under different pseudonyms. In his last book, *Poemas Clandestinos*, Dalton developed five imaginary poets—Vilma Flores, Timoteo Lúe, Jorge Cruz, Juan Zapata and Luis Luna—through whose individual personalities he spoke.

On 10 May 1975 Roque Dalton, together with a worker whose name has never been released, was assassinated by a faction of the ERP. While the circumstances surrounding his death remain obscure, it seems he fell victim to militarism and adventurism that existed at the time among the leadership of the ERP.

Roque Dalton's published works of poetry include: *La Ventana en el Rostro* (Mexico, 1961), *El Mar* (Havana, 1962), *El Turno del Ofendido* (Havana, 1963), *Los Testimonios* (Havana, 1964), *Taberna y Otros Lugares* (Havana, 1969), his historical-collage poem, *Las Historias Prohibidas del Pulgarcito* (Mexico, 1974), and *Poemas Clandestinos* (EDUCA, 1975).

His other works include a book of literary criticism, *César Vallejo*; a treatise on Debray's *Revolución en la Revolución?* entitled, *Revolucion en la Revolucion? y la critica de la derecha*; a biography written in autobiographical style called, *Miguel Marmol*; a novel published after his death, *pobrecito poeta que era yo...* (EDUCA, 1976); and two books left unpublished, *El amor me cae más mal que la primavera* and *El libro rojo de Lenin*.

Dalton also wrote important published essays on "Culture in North Korea" (TRICONTINENTAL magazine) and on "Poetry and Militancy in Latin America" (*Casa de las Américas,* Havana. English translation by Curbstone Press, Willimantic, CT.).

R.S.

QUITO, FEBRUARY 1976:
I LIGHT THE FIRE AND BECKON IT

-1-

Evening at the home of Ivan Egüez. I start to talk about Roque Dalton.

Roque was a living absurdity who never stopped. Even now, in my memory, he's running. How did death manage to catch him?

They were going to shoot him, but four days before the execution the government fell. Another time they were about to execute him and an earthquake split the prison walls and he escaped. The dictatorships of El Salvador, the little country which was his land and which he carried tatooed all over his body, could never handle him. Death took its revenge on this fellow who had so often mocked it. In the end, it slayed him through treason: it delivered the bullets from the precise place he least expected them. For months no one really knew what had happened. Was it, wasn't it? The teletypes did not vibrate to tell the world about the assassination of this poet who was born in neither Paris nor New York.

He was the most joyful of us all. And the ugliest. There are ugly people who can at least say, "I'm ugly, but symmetrical." Not he. His face was crooked. He defended himself by saying he hadn't been born that way. That's how he'd been left, he said. First a piece of brick hit his nose when he was playing soccer, the result of a doubtful penalty call. Then a rock hit his right eye. Later, a bottle hurled by a suspicious husband. Afterward, the kicks of the Salvadoran military, who didn't understand his passion for Marxism-Leninism. Then, a mysterious beating on a corner of the Mala Strana, in Prague. A band of thugs left him on the ground with a double-fractured jaw and a concussion.

A few years later, during a military maneuver, Roque was running, gun in hand, bayonet fixed, when he fell into a hole. Waiting for him was a huge sow with her newborn piglets. The sow finished off what was left of Roque.

In July 1970 he told me, choking with laughter, the story of the pig, and he showed me an album of comics about the feats of the famous Dalton brothers, movie screen gunslingers, who had been his ancestors.

Roque's poetry was like him: loving, mocking, combative. He had courage to spare, so he didn't need to mention it.

I talk about Roque and I bring him, tonight, to the home of Ivan. None of those gathered here knew him. What does it matter? Ivan has a copy of *Taberna y otros lugares*. I used to have that book as well, back in Montevideo. Leafing through *Taberna* I fail to find a poem I perhaps imagined, but which he could well have written, about the fortune and beauty of being born in America.

Ivan, who knows the Prague tavern "Ufleka," reads a poem aloud. Luis reads a long poem or love story. The book passes from hand to hand. I select some lines that describe how lovely sudden anger can be.

-2-

We all meet death in a way that resembles us. Some of us, in silence, walking on tiptoe; others, shrinking away; others, asking forgiveness or permission. There are those who meet it arguing or demanding explanations, and there are those who make their way slugging or cursing. There are those who embrace death. Those who close their eyes; those who cry. I always thought that Roque would meet death roaring with laughter. I wonder if he could have. Wouldn't the sorrow of being murdered by those who had been your comrades have been stronger?

Then the bell rings. It is Humberto Vinueza, coming from Agustín Cueva's house. As soon as Ivan opens the door Humberto says, without receiving any explanation or asking anything, "It was a dissident faction."

"What? How?"

"Those who killed Roque Dalton. Agustín told us. In Mexico the press said . . ."

Humberto sits down with us.
We all fall silent, listening to the rain hitting the window.

Eduardo Galeano

NOTES

Nazim Hikmet (1902-1963): Communist, Turkish poet and writer, who spent much of his life in a Turkish prison for inciting workers and military cadets, who read and admired his poetry, to revolt. After 15 years in prison, he was released in a general amnesty in 1950. Less than a year later in an anti-communist government crackdown, he was forced to flee to Moscow. He spent the remainder of his life in exile, living in Moscow and Europe and traveling to Cuba, China and Tanganyika. He died in Moscow in 1963.

General Martínez: Military dictator of El Salvador from 1932 to 1944. After seizing power in a coup, his refusal to certify communist electoral victories ignited a national uprising organized by Agustín Farabundo Martí. The uprising lasted three days before it was crushed by government forces. The aftermath was a massacre that went on for weeks leaving 30,000 Indians, peasants, workers and communists dead or missing.

Otto René Castillo (1936-1967): Revolutionary guerrilla and Guatemalan poet. His political activities began in 1954 as a young student organizer. During the next ten years he was imprisoned, tortured, and exiled. Castillo returned to Guatemala from exile in 1966 and joined the F.A.R. (the Armed Revolutionary Front). In March 1967 he and his guerrilla group were ambushed and captured. He was put to death on March 19, 1967.

Camilo Torres: Colombian priest who joined up with the National Liberation Army (ELN). He died in his first encounter with the Army on February 15, 1966. After his death, the young guerrilla-priest became a martyr for the Latin American Left.

ONLY THE BEGINNING: This poem comes out of the popular saying, "To whoever robs a thief, a hundred years of pardon."

Roberto Armijo: Salvadoran poet and essayist. He is at present on the Salvadoran Armed Forces' hit-list.

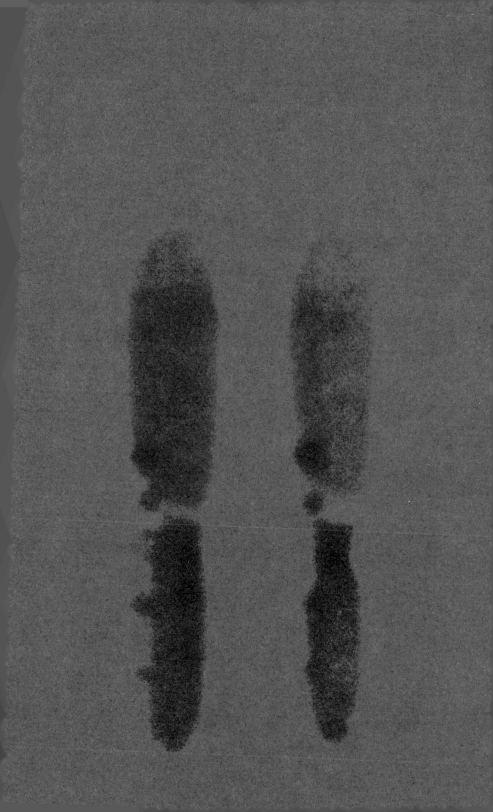

96725

PQ
7539.2
.D3
A27
1984

DALTON, ROQUE

DATE DUE